USBORNE BODY BOOKS

YOU AND YOUR
FOOD

Judy Tatchell and Dilys Wells
Designed by Nerissa Davies

CONTENTS

Illustrated by Sue Stitt, Brenda Haw, Kuo Kang Chen, Martin Newton, Stuart Trotter, Patti Pearce, Ian Jackson, Adam Willis, Sue Walliker, Chris Lyon, John Shackell and Roger Stewart.

Why do you need food?

Your whole body is made from the food you eat and all your energy comes from food. Without food you would not be able to move around, keep warm or get better when you injure yourself. You need lots of different types of food in order to feel and look good. When you have finished reading this book, you should know much more about what you eat and how it affects you. It tells you which foods are good for you, which are not so good and why.

Nutrients

Food is made up of lots of different things. Those which your body needs in order to work properly, grow and repair itself, are called nutrients.

Nutrients have different jobs, though many also work together or need the presence of others to work properly. The different types of nutrient are described on these two pages. You can find out more about all of them on the following pages.

Carbohydrate

Carbohydrate gives you energy. Bread and cereal contain a lot of carbohydrate.

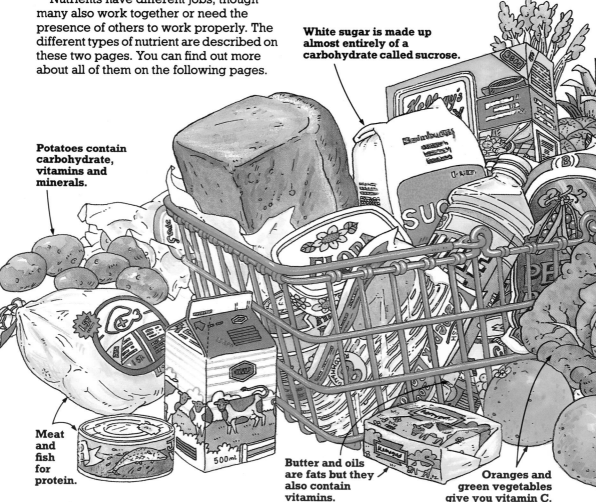

White sugar is made up almost entirely of a carbohydrate called sucrose.

Potatoes contain carbohydrate, vitamins and minerals.

Meat and fish for protein.

Butter and oils are fats but they also contain vitamins.

Oranges and green vegetables give you vitamin C.

Protein

Protein is used to build your body. Almost 20% of your weight is protein. Meat, fish and milk are good sources of protein.

Fat

Your body can store fat and use it later for energy. Meat fat, butter and oils are almost pure fat.

How do you get energy from food?

Your food comes either from animals, e.g. meat and milk, or from plants, e.g. potatoes and peas. When you have eaten and digested the food, your body can use the energy stored by the animal or plant.

Milk

Peas

Fries

Meat

Plants have to make their own food. They get the energy to do this from the sun.

When a cow eats grass, it uses the nutrients made by the grass. So the energy and nutrients you get from food such as beef and milk come first of all from plants.

Milk is made up of over 100 different nutrients.

Cheese and milk contain calcium.

Minerals

Your body needs minerals such as calcium (to help make bones and teeth) and iron (for your blood). You only need minerals in tiny quantities, though.

Vitamins

You need small amounts of about 20 nutrients called vitamins. These do different things. Vitamin C, for instance, helps glue body cells together to make firm muscles and smooth skin.

Water

You can live for several weeks without food but you will die within a few days without water. Your body is about 66% water.

Body repair

Most of the dust in your bedroom is your own dead skin cells.

Your body is made up of microscopic building blocks called cells. An adult human body has about fifty million million cells. Throughout your life cells die and are replaced with new ones, using nutrients (mainly protein) from your food. You can see this happening as a suntan fades. Tanned skin is worn away and replaced by new, lighter layers of skin underneath.

Growth and repair food

Until you are about 18, your body makes new cells in order to grow. Also, throughout your life, cells wear out and are replaced. Some types of cell only last a few weeks. Others last much longer. After seven years, each cell in an adult's body (except tooth and brain cells) has died and been replaced. All the material for new cells comes from food. Protein is the main body-building nutrient but you also need others such as vitamins and minerals. A shortage of any nutrient will weaken you and slow down growth and the rate at which you replace worn out cells.

What are proteins made of?

Proteins are made up of substances called amino acids. There are 20 types of amino acid which combine in different ways to make different proteins.

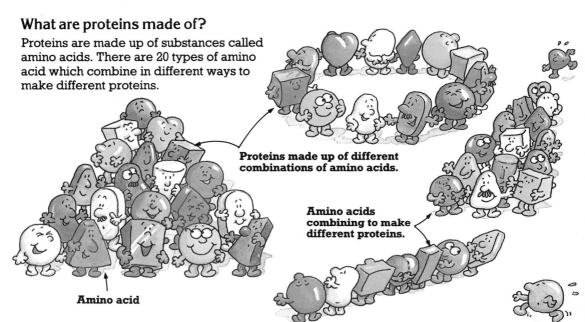

Proteins made up of different combinations of amino acids.

Amino acids combining to make different proteins.

Amino acid

Inside your digestive system*, proteins are broken down into amino acids. They can then be used to build different proteins for body tissues such as muscle, hair, skin and blood cells.

You get protein from foods which come from animals, such as meat and milk, and from plants, such as cereals, beans and nuts. A mother's milk has the very best protein. It has to provide everything a baby needs. A vegan** (someone who does not eat meat or animal products) needs a wide variety of plant proteins to provide all the necessary amino acids.

Protein per 100g of food

Roast beef	25g	(0.9oz)
Roast chicken	25g	(0.9oz)
Hard cheese	25g	(0.9oz)
Grilled cod	20g	(0.9oz)
Eggs	12g	(0.7oz)
Milk	3g	(0.1oz)
Peanuts	28g	(1.0oz)
Wholemeal bread	10g	(0.4oz)
White bread	8g	(0.3oz)
Baked beans	5g	(0.2oz)
Boiled peas	5g	(0.2oz)

Protein foods

Most food, except sugar and fat, contains some protein. Meat, fish, nuts and cheese are richest in protein. Much of your protein probably comes from foods such as bread which is only about 10% protein but which you may eat in large quantities.

A 12 year old needs about 55g (2oz) of protein a day. Here are some foods with the amount of protein in them per 100g (3.5oz).

*More about your digestive system on pages 32-33.
**More about vegans on pages 34-35.

Body building

Vitamin C helps cement your body cells together.

The way your body uses protein is similar to the way in which a builder uses bricks to build a house.

The builder cannot work unless he has enough bricks. You cannot grow unless you have enough protein.

He needs a steady supply of concrete and cement as well as bricks. Your body needs regular vitamins and minerals as well as protein.

Food for growth

Three slices of lean meat, 28g (1oz) of cheese, two slices of wholemeal bread and a large glass of milk give you enough protein for a day.

Keep your own growth chart

You may grow more quickly in the summer. Sunshine lets you make vitamin D which you need to build bones. Measure your height every month and record the readings. See if your chart shows different growth rates during the year.

Most children reach half their final adult height by their second birthday, but you grow fastest in your mid-teens. A ten year old boy usually needs at least as much food as his mother. By the age of 12 he is likely to be eating a lot more than his mother as his growth speeds up. Most girls do not grow as tall as most boys so they need slightly less food.

Measuring a pet's growth

If you have a young pet, you can compare how much it eats with how much it grows. Weigh the food you give it each day. Keep a record of your pet's age, weight and the amount of food it eats each week. Try drawing a graph to make a comparison.

How to weigh your pet:
1. Weigh yourself.
2. Weigh yourself holding pet.
3. Subtract (1) from (2).

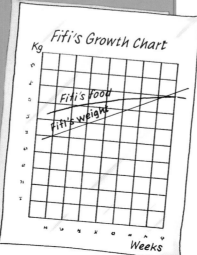

Fifi's Growth Chart

Kg

Fifi's food

Fifi's weight

Weeks

5

Energy food

You probably need more energy between the ages of 12 and 17 than at any other time in your life, because growing uses a lot of energy. Without energy you would be like a car with no petrol.

   Almost all food, except salt and water, gives you some energy The main sources are carbohydrate and fat, but you can also get energy from protein. The charts on pages 44-45 show what foods are good for energy.

Where does energy come from?

The sun's energy gets locked into plants by a process called photosynthesis during which they make their food. The word means "building up by means of light". Plants make simple sugars using water, light, gases in the air and minerals from the soil.

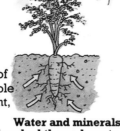

Water and minerals absorbed through roots.

When you eat an apple you can taste the sugar.

All the energy you get from food starts with the sugars made by plants. Plants use these sugars to build more complex nutrients such as proteins.

A potato stores starch to make new plants next season.

Some plants store energy for later use by combining sugars to make starch. When you eat the plant you can use the stored energy yourself. Sugar and starch are carbohydrates.

Measuring energy

Energy you get from food is measured in calories. These are the same as kilocalories (Kcal) which are used to measure heat energy in physics. Different foods provide you with different amounts of energy.

   Here, you can see roughly how many calories certain foods and drinks contain and some examples of what you can do with the energy they give you.

300 calories

Bar of chocolate

Sit a three hour exam.

Swim round a pool for 45 minutes without touching the sides.

75 calories

Slice of buttered toast

Cycle for ten minutes.

Sleep for one and a half hours.

How many calories do you need?

Some people need more calories than others, depending on how big and active they are and how efficiently their bodies use food. Between the ages of ten and 14 you probably need between 2,000 and 3,000 calories a day.

50 calories

Apple

Jog for four minutes.

Scrub the floor for five minutes.

100 calories

Glass of milk

Dance for ten minutes.

Watch TV for one and a quarter hours.

15 calories

Cup of tea

Play football for two minutes.

Walk the dog for three minutes.

How do you use your calories?

About half your calories are used for physical energy and about half for growth, breathing, digestion and so on. The more active you are, the more calories you use, though even when you are asleep your body is using energy.

Using energy foods

If you eat more carbohydrate and fat than you need for energy, or more protein than you need for growth and repair, your body stores them as fat.

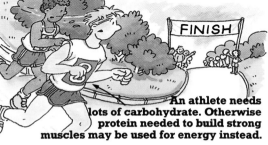

An athlete needs lots of carbohydrate. Otherwise protein needed to build strong muscles may be used for energy instead.

If you do not eat enough food to supply you with the energy you need, your body uses protein for energy instead of for growth and repair.

Vitamin spark plugs

You need certain vitamins to enable your body to release energy from the food you eat. This is similar to a car which needs a spark plug to ignite its petrol. There is more about vitamins on pages 10-11.

Starvation

If people do not get enough to eat, for instance during a famine, any food they do eat is used for energy to stay alive. This is why starving children do not grow. If they do not get enough energy from food, they start using protein from their flesh and muscles, so they waste away.

Energy stores

Your body stores energy for later use in the form of fat. Fat is a very concentrated source of energy. Weight for weight, it provides twice as much energy as carbohydrate or protein. However, too much fat is bad for you, as shown on these pages, so it is better to eat carbohydrate for energy.

Fat for survival

Fat makes up between 20% and 30% of a young woman's body weight and between 10% and 15% of a young man's.

Females have more fat on their bodies than males. This may be nature's way of making sure that in times of food shortage enough women survive to have children.

Do you need fat?

Carrying around extra fat means your heart has to work harder.

You need some body fat to cushion your internal organs, protect your bones and provide an insulating layer round you like a thin blanket. If you eat too much fat, this blanket becomes like an over-stuffed duvet.

Fats are made from substances called fatty acids. Some of these are needed for growth, healthy skin and resistance to infection. Vitamins A and D occur only in certain fats, but your body can make vitamin D itself in sunlight.*

Different types of fat

A fat molecule consists of carbon atoms in a chain. Each carbon atom has two free "arms" which can bond to hydrogen atoms. If they do not join to hydrogen atoms, they make double or triple bonds with next door carbon atoms. In a saturated fat, each carbon atom joins to two hydrogen atoms. A polyunsaturated fat has two or more multiple bonds. Saturated fats can be bad for your heart (see opposite).

Part of a saturated fat molecule.

C = carbon atom
H = hydrogen atom

Part of a polyunsaturated fat molecule.

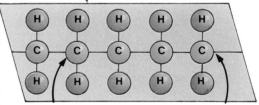

Carbon atoms bond with four separate atoms – the carbon atoms next to it and two hydrogen atoms.

Carbon atoms in a chain.

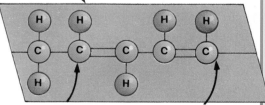

Where a carbon atom does not bond to four separate atoms, it makes double or even triple bonds.

Carbon atoms in a chain.

Saturated fats, such as lard, suet, meat fat and butter, are those which mainly come from animals. They are solid at room temperature.

Polyunsaturated fats, such as corn (maize) oil, sunflower oil and soya bean oil come from plants. They are liquid at room temperature.

8

*There is more about these vitamins on pages 10-11.

Feeling full

It is tempting to eat a lot of fatty food because when you are hungry it is very satisfying. The reason for this is that you digest fat quite slowly, so it sits in your stomach for a long time, making you feel full.

Fat and heart disease

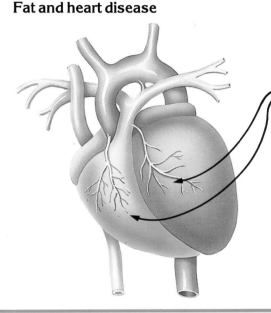

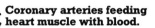

Coronary arteries feeding heart muscle with blood.

All animal foods contain a fatty substance called cholesterol. Your body also makes its own. A diet containing a lot of saturated fat can raise the amount of cholesterol in your blood to dangerous levels. A fatty substance is laid down in your arteries making them narrow.

If a blood clot gets stuck in a narrowed artery leading to the heart muscle, blocking it completely, the heart muscle is starved of blood and cannot pump properly. It may even cause the heart to stop.

Hidden fats

Some foods, such as butter and cooking oils, are obviously very fatty. A lot of other foods contain fat which is not so obvious. Here are some foods with their percentage fat content and the amounts of saturated and polyunsaturated fat they contain. The rest of the fat in them is another type of fat called unsaturated fat. In an unsaturated fat molecule, there is only one double bond.

Total percentage of fat in food.		% of fat which is saturated.	% of fat which is polyunsaturated.
Beef	21%	45%	5%
Eggs	11%	38%	13%
Salted peanuts	49%	21%	30%
Milk chocolate	30%	62%	4%
Hard cheese	34%	63%	3%
Butter	82%	63%	3%
Polyunsaturated margarine	81%	16%	54%

Cutting down on fat

Most people eat too much fat. Here are some ways to cut down.

★ Avoid spreading butter or margarine thickly.

★ Cut fat off meat before cooking. White meat, fish and poultry have less fat than red meat.

★ Grill food, don't fry it.

★ Drink skimmed milk instead of full fat milk.

★ Eat natural yoghurt instead of cream.

★ Look for low-fat cheese.

9

Vitamins

Vitamins are substances in food which you must have in order to be healthy. You only need them in small quantities and you are unlikely to go short if you eat a range of different foods.* There are about 20 vitamins. The most important ones, and what they do, are described on these pages. The chart on page 46 shows where they occur.

Vitamin A

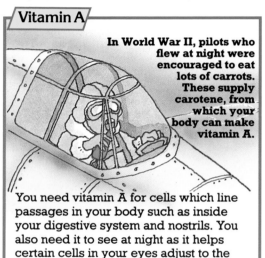

In World War II, pilots who flew at night were encouraged to eat lots of carrots. These supply carotene, from which your body can make vitamin A.

You need vitamin A for cells which line passages in your body such as inside your digestive system and nostrils. You also need it to see at night as it helps certain cells in your eyes adjust to the dark.

Vitamin C

This vitamin is important for skin, blood and general body maintenance. It is also necessary for healthy healing after an injury; for instance, to help form scar tissue.

B group vitamins

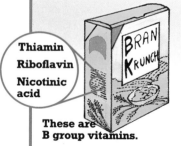

Thiamin
Riboflavin
Nicotinic acid

These are B group vitamins.

Some cereals are advertised as having added vitamins. These replace those lost during manufacture. Meat, cereals, bread, eggs and milk are the main sources of B vitamins.

The B group vitamins were originally thought to be one substance. It was then discovered that there are at least twelve different substances involved. Some B vitamins help release energy from food. Others help to make healthy blood and nerves.

Extra vitamin B6 may help women who get depressed and tense before their periods. Doctors do not know why this is, but it seems to work.

Vitamin D – the sunlight vitamin

Many old paintings show babies with rickets, so it must have been a common disease.

Some Ancient Egyptians suffered from rickets. 5,000 year old skeletons found in the Pyramids had bent bones.

You need vitamin D for strong bones. Your body makes it when sunlight falls on your skin. Adults can make all they need but growing children need extra from foods such as eggs, margarine and oily fish e.g. sardines. If they do not get enough, their bones do not harden properly and become bent. This is called rickets.

*People with coeliac disease may have vitamin deficiences. See page 41.

In the 18th century, more sailors died of vitamin C deficiency, called scurvy, than were drowned or killed in battle.

HISTORY BOOK

Vitamin C is found in citrus fruits (e.g. oranges and lemons), soft fruits, green vegetables, potatoes and tomatoes.

A few centuries ago, nearly everyone went short of vitamin C in the winter when fresh fruit and vegetables were out of season. Nowadays these foods can be frozen, imported from other countries or grown in greenhouses in the winter.

Vitamin E

This vitamin protects other valuable body chemicals. It also makes your blood more efficient in carrying oxygen around your body.

Oxygen

Vitamin K

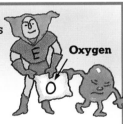

You need vitamin K to help your blood clot. Without it you would bleed to death when you cut yourself. Your body can make a certain amount of this vitamin itself and it is rare to be deficient.

Vitamin C and the common cold

Some people believe that if you take a massive dose of vitamin C each day, the same as eating 12 oranges, you will not catch colds.

Unfortunately, this has not been proved. Instead, it has been shown that large doses of vitamin C taken regularly are bad for you.

Do you need vitamin pills?

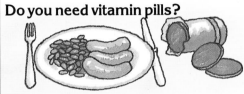

If you only ate sausages, beans and chocolate biscuits you would run short of vitamins.

You are unlikely to need vitamin pills regularly unless you only eat a limited range of food e.g. if you are on certain sorts of diet.* You may need them during or after a long illness when you cannot eat or do not want proper meals. Also, some drugs, such as aspirin, destroy vitamin C.

Too many vitamins

Eskimos do not eat polar bear's liver as it has so much vitamin A it makes them ill.

If you eat more vitamins than you need, you get rid of some of them when you go to the toilet. Your body stores the rest. If you regularly eat large quantities of vitamins, these stores can get dangerously high. This is extremely unlikely to happen unless you take massive doses of vitamin pills.

11

*There is more about safe dieting on pages 42-43.

Minerals

Minerals such as iron, calcium and salt are present in the soil. Plants absorb minerals through their roots. Because you only need small quantities of minerals you are unlikely to run short of them as long as your diet is varied.

You need about 20 different minerals. Some work with vitamins or proteins. Here are the four main reasons why you need them.

1 Building bones and teeth

Bones consist of a mesh of protein and water, filled in with hard calcium phosphate. This is made up of two materials – calcium and a little phosphorus. Calcium is found mainly in milk, cheese, cereals and vegetables. You also need vitamin D to make bones.

Close-up of bone

Bone

Air spaces to make bone lighter.

Protein, water and calcium phosphate.

Teeth are made up mainly of calcium but you need another mineral called fluoride for the enamel coating. Fluoride is found in the water supply in some places and is added to it in others to help prevent tooth decay.* Tea and fish contain fluoride.

Enamel is the hardest material in your body.

Cross-section through tooth.

12 year olds need about 700mg (0.02oz) of calcium a day. This is roughly the amount in three glasses of milk, 16 large slices of bread, four plates of spinach or 85g (3oz) of hard cheese. You get your calcium from a mixture of different foods, though.

A new baby's bones are quite soft. Calcium to harden them comes from milk in the first few years of life.

A man's body contains about 1,200g (2.5lb) of calcium. This is the amount of calcium found in 1,065 litres (1,875 pints) of milk or 148kg (326lbs) of cheese.

2 Blood

You need iron for the substance which colours your blood red and carries oxygen round your body. This is called haemoglobin and it is made of protein and iron.

Black treacle
Cocoa powder
Pig's liver
Curry powder

The foods above contain a lot of iron, but you probably do not eat them very often, and only in small quantities.

113g. (4oz) roast beef
57g. (2oz) wholemeal bread
113g. (4oz) digestive biscuits
28g. (1oz) iron enriched cereal
85g (3oz) beefburgers
142g. (5oz) beef sausages
198g. (7oz) pork sausages
71g. (2.5oz) sardines
113g. (4oz) peanuts
57g. (2oz) almonds
85g. (3oz) baked beans on toast
43g. (1.5oz) dried figs

A 12 year old needs about 12mg (0.0004oz) of iron a day. Any six of the above things will supply this. These foods contain less iron than those at the top of the list, but you probably eat more of them.

For healthy blood, you also need the minerals cobalt and copper.

*There is more about tooth decay on page 39.

Iron deficiency

The mineral you are most likely to run short of is iron. Substances in plant cells, and therefore in your food, can prevent your body from using it.

Vitamin C helps you absorb iron. Here are some suggestions for meals which contain both.

Grilled liver (iron) and cabbage (vitamin C) for supper.

Orange juice (vitamin C) and a boiled egg (iron) for breakfast.

Iron deficiency causes anaemia. It makes you feel tired and listless. You can get iron pills from a doctor. Never take more than the prescribed dose, though, as too much iron can be bad for you.

Trace elements

These are minerals which you need in minute quantities, such as selenium, chromium, molybdenum and silicon. There is very little risk of deficiency.

3 Cell regulation

Minerals such as common salt (sodium chloride), potassium, magnesium and phosphorus are needed to keep the balance of chemicals in your body cells at the correct level. These are found in many foods and there is little danger of running short.

Salt

You lose salt through your skin when you sweat. Most people eat three or four times as much salt as they need by adding it to food during cooking and before eating, and eating snacks such as salted peanuts. Excess salt can be harmful for some people. There is more about this on page 19.

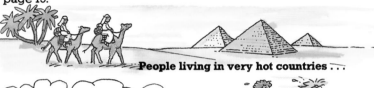

People living in very hot countries . . .

or working in very hot surroundings . . .

or long distance runners may need more salt than usual because they sweat a lot.

4 Body management

You need iodine, manganese and zinc to control certain chemical reactions that take place in your body.

Iodine is found in fish. It is also added to some brands of table salt.

Zinc comes from wholegrain cereals, peas, beans, lentils and meat.

Manganese comes from wholegrain cereals, leafy vegetables, tea and nuts.

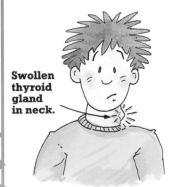

Swollen thyroid gland in neck.

Iodine helps make thyroxin which controls the rate at which energy is released from food. A shortage of iodine causes the thyroid gland in the neck to swell up. This is called goitre.

Fish is a major source of iodine. Goitre used to be common in inland areas before there were quick ways of transporting fish around a country.

13

Why do you need fibre?

Fibre is very important in your diet, although it does not contain any nutrients. It is material found in plants and which you cannot digest. You need it to add bulk to food so that your gut has something to grip onto when moving food along inside you.

What is fibre?

A plant without cellulose would be like you without your skeleton.

The main type of fibre is a substance called cellulose found in every plant cell. Plants need it to stiffen their stems and hold their leaves out flat. The tough layers round grains of wheat are a type of cellulose called bran.

Roughage and smoothage

Extra pectin is added to jam and marmalade to make it set.

Fibre used to be called roughage, because a lot of fibre foods are coarse and bulky. This is not a good name, though, as some types of fibre, such as pectin found in fruit and vegetables, are quite gluey. This type of fibre absorbs water as it passes through you.

Fibre and constipation

Fibre foods are natural laxatives.

BRAN LENTILS BROWN RICE

In the UK, about 26 million pounds a year are spent by the National Health Service on medicines to cure constipation. These medicines are called laxatives. You can avoid getting constipated by eating more fibre.

Eating more fibre

Here are some ways to increase the amount of fibre you eat. High fibre foods are satisfying as they make you feel full without making you fat.

You can buy bran to sprinkle on cereal, or eat high fibre cereals.

Cook with wholemeal flour instead of white flour. Wholemeal flour is made from the whole grain including the bran. White flour has about three-quarters of the bran removed.

Wholemeal bread is made with wholemeal flour.

Ordinary brown bread and wheatmeal bread may have had some of the bran removed.

Eat wholemeal pasta instead of white pasta.

Brown rice consists of the whole grain including the bran. White rice has had the outer layers of bran removed.

Peas, beans, nuts and dried fruit contain a lot of fibre.

Vegetables and fruit contain fibre, but they mainly consist of water.

Most people get a lot of fibre from potatoes as they tend to eat them regularly.

Water

Two-thirds of your body is water. Each of your body cells contains water. Your blood is water with minerals, proteins and blood cells floating in it. All the tubes inside you, such as your nostrils, your digestive system and lungs, are moist.

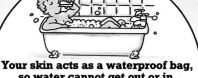

Your skin acts as a waterproof bag, so water cannot get out or in.

Getting thirsty

Salty food makes you thirsty because you need water to dissolve the salt and wash the excess out of your system in urine. Salty snacks are sold in bars to make people buy more drinks.

You can see clouds of water droplets when you breathe out on a cold day.

How much water?

You take in about two litres (three and a half pints) of water a day. One litre comes from drinks and another litre from food. Even dry food like flour and cereals contain some water. You lose about a litre of water a day in urine, and another litre in your sweat and in your breath.

Some bottled water is slightly fizzy. It tastes good with fresh orange juice.

Bottled water

You can buy bottled water which comes from deep underground springs. It contains minerals and is very pure. You need bottled water in some very hot countries where the water supply is not pure enough to drink.

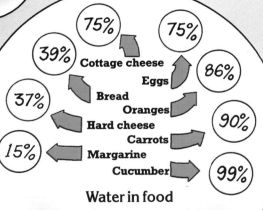

75%	75%
39% Cottage cheese	86%
Eggs	
37% Bread	
Oranges	90%
Hard cheese	
Carrots	
15% Margarine	99%
Cucumber	

Water in food

Food contains more water than you might think. This chart shows the percentage of water in some foods.

Hard and soft water

Hard water contains a lot of calcium. Soft water contains less calcium. Hard water can supply some of your calcium unless you boil it as this gets rid of minerals.

You need to use more soap in a hard water area than in a soft water area.

Healthy eating

How do you know whether you are eating enough of the right kinds of food to supply you with all your daily needs? Generally, if you eat a variety of different kinds of food you will be fine. Below, there are some guidelines to help you choose what to eat. On these two pages you can find out why the guidelines make sense if you want to eat healthily.

Guidelines for eating

★ Buy fresh food rather than ready-prepared, canned and frozen food.
★ Eat lots of different kinds of food.
★ Eat until you are comfortably full – not stuffed with food.
★ Avoid fatty meals and sweet or salty snacks.
★ Do not eat too many sweet foods.

Processed food

What would your great grandmother have thought of these foods?

Canned soup   Freeze dried beef curry.   Cream in an aerosol can.

Boil-in-the-bag fish.   Powdered mashed potato.

When your great grandparents were young, most food was eaten fresh. Nowadays, you can buy almost any food frozen, canned or packaged in some way so it can be kept for a certain time before you eat it. You can even get scrambled egg powder which keeps for months. Although they might be convenient to use, a lot of foods lose some nutrients during processing.

Choosing meals

Eating a mixture of foods will give you different nutrients. These pictures show what Nick eats during the day, and how he gets a good supply of nutrients.

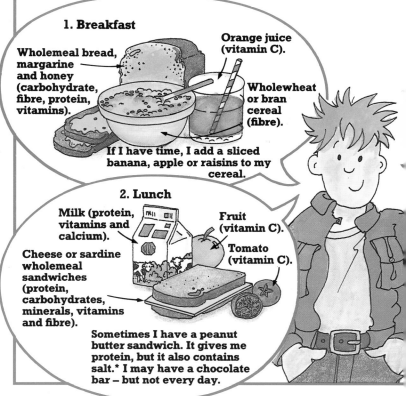

1. Breakfast

Wholemeal bread, margarine and honey (carbohydrate, fibre, protein, vitamins).

Orange juice (vitamin C).

Wholewheat or bran cereal (fibre).

If I have time, I add a sliced banana, apple or raisins to my cereal.

2. Lunch

Milk (protein, vitamins and calcium).

Fruit (vitamin C).

Tomato (vitamin C).

Cheese or sardine wholemeal sandwiches (protein, carbohydrates, minerals, vitamins and fibre).

Sometimes I have a peanut butter sandwich. It gives me protein, but it also contains salt.* I may have a chocolate bar – but not every day.

A lot of food is made to look appealing rather than to be nutritious e.g. highly coloured, artificially flavoured fizzy drinks, instant desserts, sweets, ready-cooked cakes and biscuits.

You can find out more about these kinds of food on pages 26-27.

*There is more about salt on page 19.

3. Tea

When I get home, I have a cup of tea and some nuts and raisins. These are better than peanuts or crisps which contain a lot of salt.

4. Supper

Meat (protein, vitamins and iron).

Potatoes (carbohydrate, vitamin C).

Vegetables (minerals, vitamins).

Yoghurt and fresh fruit (protein and vitamins).

If I fancy a change from meat, I have a vegetarian meal such as a bean hot pot or a nut stew for protein.

We sometimes have pasta or rice to give us carbohydrate and fill us up. But unlike potatoes, they don't contain vitamin C.

Eating the right amount

A glass of milk would stop my stomach growling.

I eat a banana, some dried fruit, or a large raw carrot to tide me over till my next meal.

If you always carry on eating when you feel full, you will probably get fat.

When you feel hungry, your body is telling you it needs food. It does not tell you what to eat, though. Sweets between meals will stop you feeling hungry but they are not good for you.

Food quantities

Here you can see how much you can eat of different foods to get enough nutrients, without too much fat, sugar, salt etc.

EAT AS MUCH AS YOU LIKE . . .

Vegetables except potatoes, dried peas, beans and lentils.

Fresh fruit.

Salad vegetables (without dressing).

Cottage cheese.

White fish (not fried).

Natural unsweetened yoghurt.

EAT IN MODERATION . . .

Lean red meat and white meat such as chicken.

Hard cheese (not cream cheese).

Eggs and milk.

Fat fish such as mackerel, sardines.

Bread, pasta, rice, potatoes (not chips).

Dried peas, beans and lentils.

Dried, canned, stewed or baked fruit.

Ice cream.

Cereals (especially sweetened ones) and nuts.

Unsweetened fruit juices.

EAT ONLY A LITTLE . . .

Butter, margarine, lard, oils.

Fried food.

Sugar, sweets, chocolate.

Jam, honey, marmalade, syrup and treacle.

Salty snacks such as peanuts.

Fat meat, including sausages and meat pies.

Biscuits, rich cakes, pastries.

Sweet and fizzy drinks.

17

*You can find out about vegetarianism on pages 34-35.

Things to avoid

Nowadays, doctors can treat many more diseases than they could a few centuries ago and people live 20 or 30 years longer. In spite of this, more people die from heart disease. This is because diets have changed and some of the things people eat are bad for them in the long term. What you eat when you are young affects your health as you get older. Some things are best avoided as far as possible. Here, you can find out why.

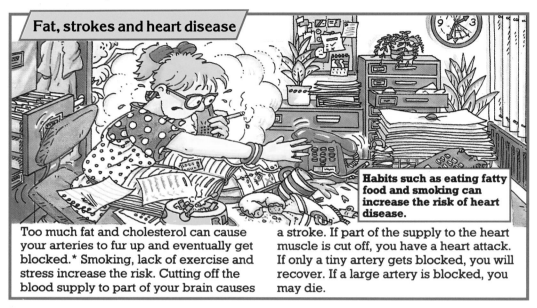

Fat, strokes and heart disease

Habits such as eating fatty food and smoking can increase the risk of heart disease.

Too much fat and cholesterol can cause your arteries to fur up and eventually get blocked.* Smoking, lack of exercise and stress increase the risk. Cutting off the blood supply to part of your brain causes a stroke. If part of the supply to the heart muscle is cut off, you have a heart attack. If only a tiny artery gets blocked, you will recover. If a large artery is blocked, you may die.

What is wrong with sugar?

Even if you cut out all these sweet snacks . . .

. . . you would still eat lots of sugar in these foods.

Although sugar gives you energy, it has almost no other nutrients besides carbohydrate. If you eat too much sugary food, your teeth are likely to rot and you may put on weight. Instead, you can get plenty of energy from food which contains other nutrients as well as carbohydrate.

Being overweight

When you carry a heavy suitcase, your heart beats faster as it has to work harder. Some people carry around this extra weight all the time as fat on their bodies. This puts a constant strain on their hearts. Some people are naturally fatter than others. Unless you are over your natural weight, your heart will not suffer.

18

*There is more about this on page 9.

What is wrong with salt?

If you stop adding salt to your food and cut down on salty snacks, you will begin to notice the taste of salt in ready-prepared and packaged food.

Most people eat at least twice as much as they need. There is a lot of salt in packaged foods. Nearly all breakfast cereals contain some salt for flavouring. In certain people, too much salt raises blood pressure, which puts a strain on their hearts. In case salt affects you in this way, it is best to cut down on it as much as possible.

Caffeine

I need a cup of coffee first thing in the morning to get me going.

I'm dying for a cup of tea.

Caffeine is found in coffee*, tea and cola drinks. It is a stimulant, which means that it makes your heart beat faster and perks you up. The effect of a cup of tea or coffee can last for up to three hours. In large quantities it can harm your stomach lining. It can also put a strain on small children's hearts.

Coffee last thing at night stops me sleeping.

Changing your eating habits

Here are some ways in which you can adjust your eating habits so you are more likely to stay healthy as you get older.

Less fat   Eat less meat, cream, cheese, butter, margarine, cakes, biscuits, fried food, chocolate and other fatty foods.

More fibre   Eat wholemeal bread and pasta, potatoes, more vegetables, salads and fruit.

Less sugar   Cut down on sweets, cakes, sweetened drinks and other sugary things.

Less salt   Cut down on salty snacks, packaged food flavoured with salt, and salt you add to food you are cooking or at the table.

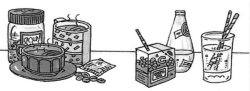

Less tea and coffee   One or two cups a day will do no harm. Drink unsweetened fruit juices and spa water instead. You can try different herb and fruit "teas", too.

You can buy coffee with most of the caffeine removed, called decaffeinated coffee.

Eating habits

By the age of two, you have developed tastes in food which influence what you enjoy eating throughout your life. You can adjust your eating habits, though, if you do not think you eat healthily enough. The main things to remember are to eat regular meals consisting of a wide variety of food in not too huge quantities.

Meals to suit your lifestyle

Most people nowadays need less food than their ancestors because they use up less energy.

People travel around in cars and buses instead of walking . . .

. . . and do less physical jobs.

Many people only have one full meal a day and make do with snacks and light meals the rest of the time. On the right are some ideas for snack meals which are easy to prepare.

Breakfast

After a night without any food at all, your body's batteries need recharging. If you have some breakfast, you will have more energy and be more alert.

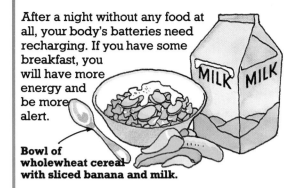

Bowl of wholewheat cereal with sliced banana and milk.

Muesli with grated apple.

Snack lunches

Here are some ideas for quick mid-day meals at home.

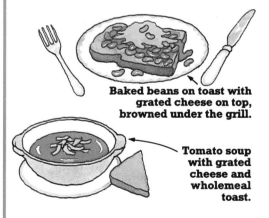

Baked beans on toast with grated cheese on top, browned under the grill.

Tomato soup with grated cheese and wholemeal toast.

Between-meal snacks

According to research, most people eat a snack of some sort six times during the day. You only need snacks in addition to good, regular meals if you are very physically active, or if you are growing quickly. Make sure snacks do not take away your appetite for more nutritious meals.

Here are some snack drinks you can make up in a couple of minutes.

Natural yoghurt, with chopped dates and honey.

Bacon sandwich

Wholemeal roll with slice of cold ham.

Easy pizza – French bread sliced lengthways, topped with cheese, grilled tomato and ham.

Pilchards or sardines on toast with sliced tomato.

Cottage cheese on rye crispbread with chopped nuts and raisins.

Cold milk whisked into fruit yoghurt.

A whole egg beaten into a glass of fresh, unsweetened orange juice.

On average, a third of the population in the UK eats or drinks something each hour between the hours of 6.45am and midnight.

Likes and dislikes

Food habits are formed at a young age, so small children should be fed as many different kinds of food as possible. If they get used to different tastes and textures, they may be less fussy about food when they get older.

Trying new things

It is fun to try new kinds of food. If you see something you have never eaten in a shop, try it. You may not like it at first, but your tastes might change as you get older.

If you go abroad, try the traditional dishes of the country. Look around shops and supermarkets to see what different food is on sale and how it is prepared.

Making changes

Giving things up or changing a habit is difficult, but there are some times when you may find it easier than others. Take advantage of a time when your normal routine is changing anyway, for instance, when you come back from a holiday, or after you have been ill.

Buying fresh food

Several changes happen to your food between the time when it is harvested or killed and when it ends up on your plate. On these two pages you can find out about choosing fresh food to buy so you can eat it at its best, when it has the most nutritional content, or food value.

Fresh vegetables and salad

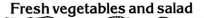

These vegetables start to wilt and lose vitamin C within hours of being picked, so they are rushed to the shops and sold while still in good condition. Good shops do not sell wilting vegetables.

These keep a little longer than leafy vegetables, but they still taste best and have the most nutrients if they are eaten soon after picking.

Soft fruit

Soft fruits such as strawberries and raspberries deteriorate very quickly. Fruit you pick yourself from a garden or fruit farm tastes much better than fruit you buy, which may have spent a day or more getting to the shops.

"Keeping" fruit and vegetables

Hard fruit such as apples and pears keep quite well for several months in a cool, dark place. Cooking apples tend to keep better than eating apples.

Fruit which needs to be grown in a different climate and imported is picked while it is unripe. It ripens slowly on the journey so it arrives in the shops in peak condition.

Root vegetables such as potatoes, carrots, turnips and onions, keep for several months in a cool, dark place. Potatoes and onions start to sprout in the light, and potatoes turn green*.

*You can find out about green potatoes on page 29.

Dairy produce

Dairy products such as milk, eggs, butter, cheese and yoghurt deteriorate quickly if they are not kept cool.

If an egg is stale, it floats. If it is bad, it smells when you break it.

Milk

Milk is heated to high temperatures in a process called pasteurization which makes it keep longer. This kills off most of the bacteria* which turn milk sour, and also any disease bacteria.

Before pasteurization and refrigeration, cows were led round cities and milked on doorsteps. Otherwise the milk would turn sour within a few hours.

Meat and fish

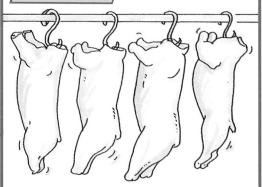

Freshly killed meat is very tough. It is usually hung in a cool place for a few days while it becomes more tender.

Fish goes off very quickly, so it is often frozen at sea. In the shops it is kept in freezer units or packed in ice on display counters.

Buying fruit and veg

★ Choose firm, bright, crisp produce. Old fruit looks dull. Green vegetables are limp and yellowy.
★ Buy them in small quantities and eat them soon afterwards.
★ Fruit and vegetables are best and cheapest in season. Out of season, they may not taste so good as they may have been grown in artificial conditions or been imported.

Buying dairy produce

★ Only buy dairy produce from shops with spotlessly clean refrigerators.
★ Never buy eggs which have been stored in a warm place. They get stale within five days when warm, but keep up to three weeks in a refrigerator.
★ Check eggs are not cracked.
★ Check the SELL BY dates on yoghurt, butter, cheese and so on.

Buying meat and fish

★ Do not buy meat or fish from a shop that is not extremely clean.
★ Avoid packages of frozen meat that contain lumps of ice or liquid that has seeped out and refrozen. If it has defrosted and refrozen, bacteria may have grown.
★ Check fish is firm and moist, the eyes clear and not sunken, the gills bright red and that it smells good.

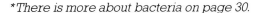

*There is more about bacteria on page 30.

Packaged and preserved food

To stop food going bad, it usually needs to be treated in some way. It also needs packaging to stop it getting contaminated. Most supermarkets are full of packaged food; either frozen or in tins, jars, tubes or cartons. Here you can find out about how food is preserved and packaged, and whether it affects the nutritional content, or food value.

Why preserve food?

Your food also provides food for microscopic creatures called microbes, such as moulds, yeasts and bacteria. These are present in small, harmless quantities in or on fresh food. In time they multiply.

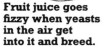

Fruit juice goes fizzy when yeasts in the air get into it and breed.
As they feed, they break down the food, making it taste and smell bad. They can be dangerous in large quantities as they or their waste products are poisonous.

Bacteria on meat multiply and make it smell bad.

Methods of preserving food kill microbes or slow down their activity.
Below you can see what happens to a loaf of bread if it gets left uneaten.

Harmless moulds are deliberately grown in some cheeses to give a strong flavour.

Freezing

At around body temperature, bacteria can divide every 20 minutes.

Microbes live and breed best in warm surroundings. Freezing inactivates most of them, and refrigeration slows them down. Before freezing, vegetables are plunged into boiling water for a short while to kill off microbes. This also destroys some vitamins and minerals.

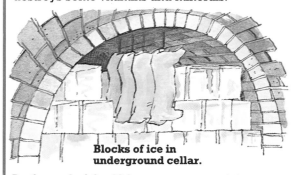

Blocks of ice in underground cellar.

By the end of the 18th century, some rich people had sorts of refrigerators. These were rooms with very thick walls called ice houses, or cold underground cellars. In winter, blocks of ice and snow were cut and put inside. The ice took a long time to melt so meat could be stored there for weeks or even months.

One day **One week** **Four weeks**

Canning

Food is heated to destroy microbes and then sealed in airtight cans to prevent other microbes getting in. Food loses more nutrients during canning than during freezing, though canned food keeps longer than frozen food.

Dent in can may allow microbes in.

Microbes have got into this can, making it bulge.

Do not buy dented cans. The dents may weaken the can and let in microbes. Bulging cans are very dangerous. They show that microbes have got in and bred.

Drying

Fish drying in the sun.

Dried food is hard on the outside, so microbes find it difficult to get in. Drying destroys most of the vitamins, but leaves protein intact, so it is better for meat than vegetables. Drying is mainly done in factories, though in some parts of the world, meat and fish are still dried in the sun or the wind.

Salt, sugar and vinegar

Salt, sugar and vinegar inactivate most microbes. They have been used to preserve food for centuries.

Nowadays, vinegar is mainly used for pickling vegetables.

Sugar is used as a preservative in jams, marmalades and sweet pickles.

Meat is covered in salt and then hung up to dry. This is called curing.

Smoked food

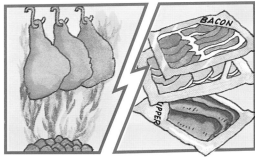

Meat and fish used to be smoked to preserve it. You can still buy food such as smoked kippers and bacon, but the smokey flavour is usually artificial and they last no longer than fresh food.

Date-stamping

To make sure food is eaten before it goes off, many dairy products, packets and frozen foods are marked with a date before which they should be used. Unopened cans last for years so they do not need date-stamping.

You should normally eat food within a couple of days of its SELL BY date.

Food additives

Food additives are substances added to food to preserve it and affect its appearance, texture, taste, smell and so on. Some are natural, such as salt and spices. Others are manufactured chemicals. You can find out here why they are added to some foods and whether they can affect you.

Preservatives

There is more about preservatives on pages 24-25.

A lot of food has preservatives added to it so it will keep on a shop shelf or in your kitchen cupboard.

Anti-oxidants

Butter left out in the warm goes rancid and develops a horrid flavour.

Oxygen in the air causes fatty foods to go off. Anti-oxidants such as vitamin E and vitamin C help to prevent this.

Flavourings

Yoghurt flavoured with real cherries (it may contain synthetic flavouring too).

Synthetically flavoured yoghurt.

Maltol is added to some packaged cakes and bread. It makes them taste and smell freshly baked.

Natural flavourings include oils from citrus fruits and spices e.g. cinnamon. Some flavourings are artificial, or synthetic. A yoghurt labelled "cherry yoghurt" must contain cherries. A yoghurt labelled "cherry flavour" may have chemicals that taste of cherries instead.

Emulsifiers and stabilizers

Stabilizers are added to instant desserts and toppings, to make them foamy when they are mixed.

An emulsifier called lecithin, found in eggs and soya beans, stops sauces such as mayonnaise from separating.

These affect the texture of a food and stop it changing during storage. Substances called polyphosphates are added to cured ham and frozen poultry, to keep them tender and juicy.

Are additives necessary?

The sweetener cyclamate, which is 30 times sweeter than sugar, was banned in the US and UK because tests indicated it might be linked to cancer.

Preservatives and anti-oxidants are necessary to stop food going off. For instance, they make meat products safe to eat if you cannot buy and eat fresh meat. Others, such as food colourings, are less vital as they only affect the look of a food.

Are additives safe?

Some people suffer from dizziness and headaches after eating meals with a lot of monosodium glutamate. This is called Chinese Restaurant Syndrome, as it is used a lot in Chinese cooking.

Many additives used in food are natural e.g. chlorophyll (green), paprika (red) and saffron (yellow). Others are synthetic. All additives are tested before they can be used, but some may have long-term effects not yet known. It is probably best to eat as much fresh, additive-free food as possible. Fresh food is usually more nutritious, anyway.

Food colouring

Fizzy orange drink with artificial colour and flavour – no oranges.

Colouring is added to some foods which lose their natural colour during processing. Others are coloured to make them look as if they contain ingredients which they do not, or just to make them look more attractive.

Sweeteners

Sugar acts as a preservative as well as a sweetener e.g. in jams.

Sugar is added to a lot of food. Other sweeteners such as saccharin are more concentrated. They contain almost no calories and so are put in diet drinks and low calorie foods.

Flavour enhancers

Flavour enhancers can be used when flavour is lost during processing.

Flavour enhancers, such as salt* and monosodium glutamate, strengthen flavour. Salt only works as a flavour enhancer in small quantities. In large quantities, it just makes things taste salty.

Anti-caking and firming agents

Anti-caking agents are added to foods such as icing sugar and powdered milk to stop them clogging up. Firming agents made from pectin are added to some fruit and vegetables during processing to prevent them going soft.

Adding nutrients

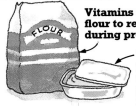

Vitamins are added to white flour to replace those lost during processing.

Vitamins are added to margarine so that it contains as many as butter, if not more.

Some foods have nutrients added to them. Vitamins A and D have to be added to margarine by law. When cereals are processed to make breakfast foods, they are heated to very high temperatures which destroys some vitamins. Most manufacturers replace them afterwards.

Allergies and hyperactivity

There are very strict regulations about what can be added to baby foods, in case of side effects or allergies.

Some people are allergic to additives such as tartrazine (a yellow colouring) and sodium benzoate (a preservative). Children with these allergies may be hyperactive, that is, extremely restless, disturbed and difficult. You can find out more about allergies and their symptoms on page 40.

Food labelling

Ingredients: carbonated water, mango juice, sugar, flavouring, preservative E211, colouring E102.

Most countries have food labelling laws stating what a manufacturer must say about the ingredients in packaged food.
In EEC countries, all ingredients must be listed in order of weight. Additives other than flavourings have an E number, e.g. E236 for the preservative formic acid. Flavourings just have numbers e.g. 621 for monosodium glutamate. Some books on nutrition have lists of what the numbers stand for and any known side effects.

See pages 18-19 for more about salt.

Storing, preparing and cooking food

Have you ever thought why you cook food? Raw meat is very tough and chewy and you would probably not like the taste. Baked bread and cakes taste nicer than the flour and raw eggs they are made from. Cooking kills dangerous microbes which might be present. It also breaks down the tough cellulose in plant cells so you can digest vegetables more easily.

Cooking can destroy valuable nutrients, though. So can the way you store and prepare food. Here, you can find out what to do about it.

Dissolving nutrients

Vitamin C, some B group vitamins and some minerals dissolve in water during washing and boiling.

Cooking vegetables in shallow water washes fewer nutrients out. Put on a tight fitting lid so any uncovered bits cook in the steam.

Water in which you have cooked vegetables, and meat juices that have dripped out during cooking, can be used to make gravy, soup or sauces.

Putting vegetables into boiling water reduces cooking time and fewer nutrients are destroyed. You may need to start old potatoes in cold water, though, to stop them breaking up. Potatoes have a lot of nutrients in their skins, so you can scrub them instead of peeling them.

Wash and boil vegetables in large pieces. More nutrients get washed out of small bits. Tearing lettuce and cabbage leaves instead of cutting them means they separate along the edges of the cells so fewer nutrients seep out.

Keeping meals hot in the oven destroys some of their goodness.

Rinse vegetables and meat instead of soaking them, except where meat has to be soaked to reduce saltiness e.g. salted ham or bacon.

When you toast bread, between 10% and 30% of its thiamin (a B vitamin) is lost.

Vitamins destroyed by heat

Vitamin C and some B vitamins are destroyed by heat. Do not overcook vegetables as they go soggy and bitter as well as losing vitamins.

Vitamins destroyed by light

Vitamins A, C and some B vitamins are broken down by bright light.

Storing food in a refrigerator keeps it cool and in the dark. It preserves vitamins destroyed by light as well as stopping food from going off.

Keep milk in the refrigerator. If left out in the sun, its riboflavin (a B vitamin) is destroyed. It also goes sour.

Covering bowls of food with polythene will stop them drying out or passing their flavours on to other food.

Food cooks very quickly in a microwave oven, losing few vitamins.

Bananas go brown in the refrigerator, so keep them in a cool, dark place instead.

Root vegetables, such as potatoes, carrots, and swedes should be kept in a cool, dark place. New potatoes get a sweet taste if kept in the refrigerator.

Storing salads and leafy vegetables in the refrigerator keeps them fresher and retains nutrients.

Potatoes go green in the light. Do not eat them when they are like this as the green is a poisonous chemical.

A pressure cooker reduces cooking time by about a third. It makes water boil at a higher temperature. Vegetables cook more quickly in the hotter water and lose fewer vitamins.

Cooking to preserve vitamins

The lower the temperature at which food is cooked, the longer it takes. The longer food is cooked, the more vitamins are lost. Fast cooking at a high temperature loses fewest vitamins. Some cuts of meat need cooking for a long time, though, to make them tender; if you grill stewing steak, it is almost too tough to chew.

Chemical raising agents

Baking soda and other substances used to make bread and cakes rise destroy thiamin (a B vitamin) in the flour. A cake can lose about 80% of its thiamin during baking. A loaf of bread made with yeast only loses between 15 and 30%.

Food safety

If you have ever had food poisoning you will probably want to know how to avoid it happening again. It usually makes you very sick and you feel dreadful for a day or two. If babies, old or weak people get it, it can be more serious. It is caused by harmful bacteria which have been allowed to breed on food. These two pages will help you understand how bacteria spread, so you can reduce the risk of food poisoning.

What are bacteria?

Bacteria are microscopic creatures. Thousands could fit on a pinhead. Some live on you and inside you and are quite harmless. Others are harmful if they multiply inside you or if you eat the poisons, or toxins, which they produce. In a warm room, one bacteria can become several million within 24 hours. Here are the bacteria which are usually responsible for food poisoning.

Salmonella

These bacteria live inside most animals. They are normally killed by cooking.

Staphylococci

Staphylococci may exist quite harmlessly in your nose, throat and ears. They are also present in infected cuts, boils and sores. They produce a toxin which causes food poisoning.

Clostridium botulinum

Just 225g (8oz) of the toxin produced by these bacteria would be enough to kill the whole population of the world.

These bacteria produce a very poisonous toxin in low acid conditions where there is no oxygen. Because food cans provide those conditions, canning involves heating food to temperatures which are known to kill bacteria. Botulism (the disease caused by the toxin) is extremely rare.

Stopping the spread

Everything that comes into contact with food should be very clean. The pictures on these pages show where bacteria can thrive in a kitchen. Read the hints to find out how you can reduce the risk of food poisoning.

Wash dishcloths, tea and hand towels frequently.

The kitchen sink should be kept clean and disinfected and should be used only for preparing food and washing up.

Keep meat, poultry and fish covered in the refrigerator.

Prevent flies, other insects and mice from coming in contact with food.

More hints to avoid food poisoning

Meat cooked on one day and eaten on another must be thoroughly reheated before being served to kill salmonella.

Wash your hands after removing the giblets from poultry. They will have lots of salmonella bacteria on them.

Cover cuts with clean dressings.

Wash your hands before touching food. Handle cooked and prepared food as little as possible.

CHOO!!

Do not sneeze on food and, if possible, avoid preparing it when you have a cold.

Keep pets, pet food and pets' dishes away from your food.

Keep raw and cooked meat separate to avoid contamination. Standing raw meat on a board may leave harmful bacteria on it. If you then chop food on the board without scrubbing it first, the bacteria may infect it.

Chicken and meat should be eaten within three days of purchase. Cooked stews, pies and gravy should be eaten within two days.

PURR...

Keep all kitchen utensils and everything that comes into contact with food clean.

Line rubbish bins with disposable bags. Empty and disinfect bins regularly.

Wash your hands well with soap after going to the toilet, changing a baby's nappy, clearing up an animal's mess or cleaning out a pet's cage. These are very common causes of food poisoning due to salmonella bacteria.

Use a lot of soapy water for washing up. Rinse everything in clean, hot water and leave things to drain. Bacteria can breed on dirty dish towels. A washing-up machine is hygienic as it uses hotter water than you can when washing by hand.

Defrost meat thoroughly before cooking. If it is still frozen in the middle when it is put into the oven, it may not cook all the way through. You need to be especially careful with large poultry – it can take a whole day to defrost completely.

Eating and digestion

Digesting food means breaking it down into molecules which can be absorbed by your body. This process starts in your mouth and carries on all the way through you. Food travels down your gut, or alimentary canal. The top part deals with digestion, the lower part with absorption and the end part with getting rid of waste.

Digestion

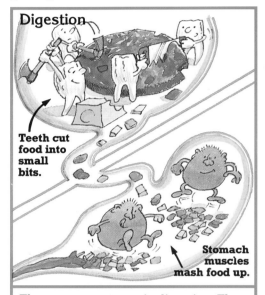

Teeth cut food into small bits.

Stomach muscles mash food up.

There are two stages in digestion. The first stage is mechanical. Your teeth cut food up into small pieces and your stomach muscles mash it.

Large food molecule

Enzyme

The other stage in digestion is chemical. Substances called enzymes in your digestive juices break large molecules of food down into smaller molecules. A complex molecule of food is like a string of beads. Different enzymes jerk the string in different places, so finally the string is broken into simple, small molecules.

Your alimentary canal

Mouth
In your mouth, your teeth grind, crush and tear food into small pieces. Your tongue mixes it with saliva, making it easier to swallow. Saliva comes from the salivary glands under your tongue and at the back of your mouth. Enzymes in your saliva start to break down starch in your food into a sugar called maltose.

Oesophagus
When you swallow food, your tongue pushes it into your oesophagus. This is a muscular tube which sends food along to your stomach with a rippling movement called peristalsis.

Stomach
Your stomach is a thick, muscular bag. It churns food around, mixing it with an acidic juice called gastric juice, until it is a creamy mixture. Enzymes in gastric juice break proteins down into smaller units called peptides.

The pyloric sphincter is a muscular ring which opens to let the liquid food mixture out of your stomach bit by bit.

Duodenum (top part of small intestine)
A juice called bile flows into the duodenum from the gall bladder. It contains salts which break down fats into small droplets. Juices from the pancreas break down proteins and peptides into amino acids, fats into fatty acids and glycerol, and starch into maltose.

Ileum (rest of small intestine)
The small intestine produces juices which finish off digestion. Peptides are broken down into amino acids and fats into fatty acids and glycerol. Maltose, sucrose and lactose are all sugars which are broken down into glucose.

Food is absorbed in your small intestine. It is about as long as a bus. The ileo caecal valve lets unabsorbed substances out into the large intestine.

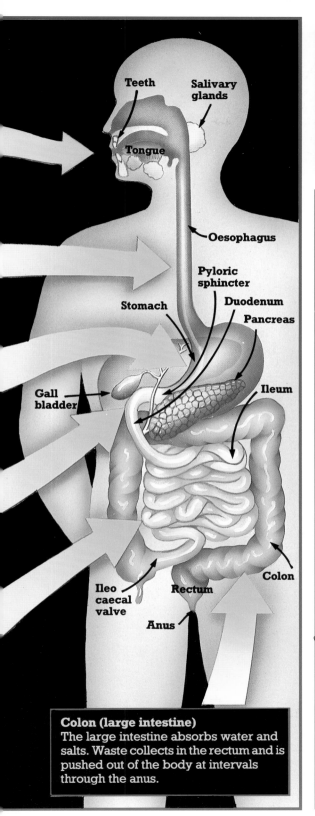

Teeth

Salivary glands

Tongue

Oesophagus

Pyloric sphincter

Stomach

Duodenum

Pancreas

Gall bladder

Ileum

Ileo caecal valve

Rectum

Colon

Anus

Colon (large intestine)
The large intestine absorbs water and salts. Waste collects in the rectum and is pushed out of the body at intervals through the anus.

Indigestion

Indigestion can be caused by too much acidic gastric juice in the stomach. You feel full and your stomach seems to burn. You might get indigestion if you eat too much, because your stomach cannot cope. If you eat very fast you swallow a lot of air. This collects in your stomach making you feel uncomfortably bloated.

How long does digestion take?

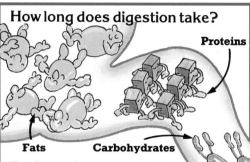

Proteins

Fats   Carbohydrates

Food stays in your stomach for between one hour and four and a half hours. Carbohydrates leave your stomach first, followed by proteins. Fats stay in your stomach the longest. A meal takes about a day to travel right the way through you.

Useful bacteria

Not all bacteria are harmful. There are about three hundred different kinds, weighing about 1.5kg (3lbs), living in your large intestine, and a smaller number in your small intestine. They destroy harmful bacteria, neutralize toxins* and produce some vitamins.

Appetite and hunger

Hunger is a physical need for food. You feel empty and your stomach may growl. Appetite is looking forward to food. It may make your mouth water. This is your saliva starting to flow.

33

*Toxins are explained on page 30.

Vegetarians and vegans

Vegetarians do not eat meat. People become vegetarians for various reasons. Some think it is wrong to kill animals for food, or object to modern farming methods in which animals are kept cramped together. Most think it makes for a healthier diet. Some are stricter than others about what they eat.

The word vegetarian comes from the Latin *vegetus* meaning whole, fresh and lively. Different kinds of vegetarianism are described on this page.

Strict vegetarians — vegans

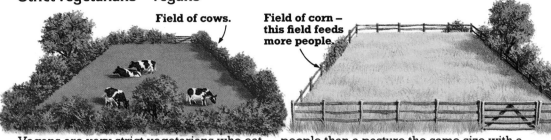

Field of cows.

Field of corn – this field feeds more people.

Vegans are very strict vegetarians who eat nothing that comes from animals. They think that rearing animals for food is a waste of land that could be used for growing crops. A field of grain feeds more people than a pasture the same size with a few cows on it. Besides meat and fish, vegans do not eat cheese, milk, eggs, butter, lard or any food in which animal products are used.

Less strict vegetarians

When you watch lambs playing in the spring, you may forget that most of them end up on a dinner plate.

Vegetarians do not make a distinction between killing a calf, say, and killing a pet.

Less strict vegetarians, called ovo-lacto vegetarians, object to animals being killed for food. They will not eat meat, fish or poultry, but they eat animal products, such as milk, which do not take the life of an animal. They eat unfertilized eggs i.e. those that will not grow into a chicken. Most eggs you buy are unfertilized.

Meat-eaters or vegetarians?

Some cattle raised for veal are fattened up in small, dark pens. This stops them moving about and keeps the meat white.

Battery hens are kept in cages, whether they are bred to lay eggs or for eating.

Some people do not eat red meat such as beef, lamb or pork. This may be because they do not like the look or feel of red meat, especially when raw. They may eat fish and even poultry, though.

Others feel it is wrong that certain animals spend all their lives cooped up being bred for food. The slaughtering process, although quick, may also be frightening. They do not feel so bad about eating fish as they can swim about freely until they are caught.

A vegetarian diet

You do not need to eat meat in order to get all your nutrients. Here are some sources of nutrients for a vegetarian.

Eggs, milk and cheese have very similar nutrients to meat and fish i.e. protein, iron, fat, vitamins A and D and B group vitamins.

Peas, beans, nuts and wholegrain cereals have protein, minerals and vitamins.

Vegetarians usually eat more fresh vegetables and fruit, and less sugary and fatty food.

A vegan diet

As vegans do not eat any meat or dairy produce, they must get all their nutrients from other sources. A vegan diet needs careful planning and should be made up of a wide selection of these foods.

Fresh and dried peas and beans.

Onion, garlic and herbs for flavouring.

Fresh and dried fruit.

Root vegetables.

Leafy vegetables.

Salad vegetables.

Textured vegetable protein in casseroles and "meat loaf" dishes.

Yeast extracts and vegetable stocks in soups.

Pasta, brown rice and wholegrain cereals.

Nuts in roasts, loaves, salads, muesli and desserts.

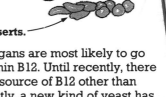

The vitamin vegans are most likely to go short of is vitamin B12. Until recently, there was no known source of B12 other than animals. Recently, a new kind of yeast has been discovered which makes vitamin B12.

Hindu vegetarians

Cows have not been killed amongst Hindus in India since the seventh century.

Hindus believe that after death your soul comes back in a different living body. If you behave badly during your life you may return as an animal, so Hindus do not eat animals.

Although Hindus will not eat beef, cow's milk and milk products are highly valued. This is because cows are regarded as sacred animals.

Health and vegetarianism

Some ovo-lactarian diets may be no more healthy than a mixed diet, as they contain a lot of dairy foods such as eggs and cheese. These are high in saturated animal fats which can be bad for your heart.*

Most vegetarians consider their diet more healthy than a meaty one, though. Here are two of their arguments.

1. Most cases of food poisoning can be traced back to meat.
2. Animals are often reared cramped together, so infections can spread easily. To limit this, animals are given lots of preventative drugs. Some of these drugs remain in the animal's flesh when it is killed and eaten.

35

*See pages 8-9.

Health foods

Health foods are thought by many people to be better for you than processed food containing additives, or refined food which may have had some of its goodness removed. Health foods include wholefoods such as wholemeal bread, wholemeal flour and wholegrain rice, and natural foods such as untreated yoghurt.

Here, you can find out more about what health foods are. They also include organically grown food. You can find out what this is at the bottom of the page.

Buying health food

Here are some foods which you may find in a health food shop. See if you can work out from the information in the picture whether they are genuinely better for you than other varieties of food.

Many ordinary supermarkets stock some health foods, at cheaper prices. In health food shops, look for foods which you cannot buy in a supermarket, such as a wide range of dried peas, beans, dried fruits, nuts, pasta and wholegrain cereal products.

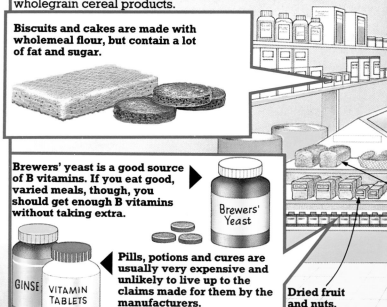

Biscuits and cakes are made with wholemeal flour, but contain a lot of fat and sugar.

Brewers' yeast is a good source of B vitamins. If you eat good, varied meals, though, you should get enough B vitamins without taking extra.

Brewers' Yeast

Pills, potions and cures are usually very expensive and unlikely to live up to the claims made for them by the manufacturers.

GINSE | VITAMIN TABLETS

Dried fruit and nuts.

Organically grown food

This is food grown without artificial (inorganic) fertilizers or chemical weedkillers and insecticides. Instead, natural (organic) fertilizers, such as farmyard manure and compost, are used.

Plants break down organic fertilizers into nitrates and phosphates before they absorb them. Inorganic fertilizers are already in this form. It is not known whether plants can tell the difference between organic and inorganic fertilizers.

Organic fertilizers improve the texture of the soil, making it easier to dig and for plants to make roots and absorb water.

Hoof and horn meal and blood meal fertilizers. Weeding is done by hand, with no chemical weedkillers.

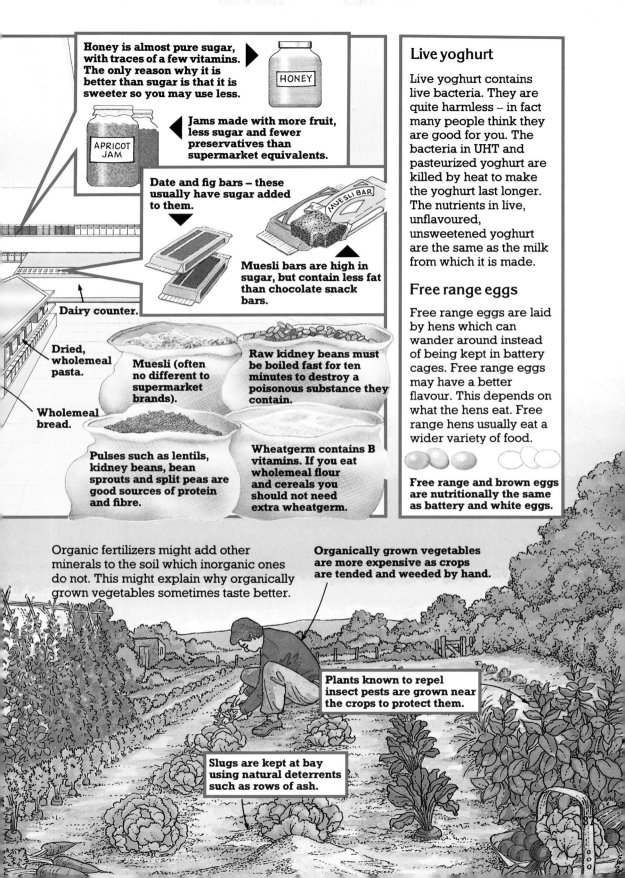

Honey is almost pure sugar, with traces of a few vitamins. The only reason why it is better than sugar is that it is sweeter so you may use less.

HONEY

Jams made with more fruit, less sugar and fewer preservatives than supermarket equivalents.

APRICOT JAM

Date and fig bars – these usually have sugar added to them.

MUESLI BAR

Muesli bars are high in sugar, but contain less fat than chocolate snack bars.

Dairy counter.

Dried, wholemeal pasta.

Muesli (often no different to supermarket brands).

Raw kidney beans must be boiled fast for ten minutes to destroy a poisonous substance they contain.

Wholemeal bread.

Pulses such as lentils, kidney beans, bean sprouts and split peas are good sources of protein and fibre.

Wheatgerm contains B vitamins. If you eat wholemeal flour and cereals you should not need extra wheatgerm.

Live yoghurt

Live yoghurt contains live bacteria. They are quite harmless – in fact many people think they are good for you. The bacteria in UHT and pasteurized yoghurt are killed by heat to make the yoghurt last longer. The nutrients in live, unflavoured, unsweetened yoghurt are the same as the milk from which it is made.

Free range eggs

Free range eggs are laid by hens which can wander around instead of being kept in battery cages. Free range eggs may have a better flavour. This depends on what the hens eat. Free range hens usually eat a wider variety of food.

Free range and brown eggs are nutritionally the same as battery and white eggs.

Organic fertilizers might add other minerals to the soil which inorganic ones do not. This might explain why organically grown vegetables sometimes taste better.

Organically grown vegetables are more expensive as crops are tended and weeded by hand.

Plants known to repel insect pests are grown near the crops to protect them.

Slugs are kept at bay using natural deterrents such as rows of ash.

Fast food

Nowadays, most towns have at least one fast food restaurant, selling pizzas, hamburgers, fried fish, chips or fries, milkshakes, cokes, coffees etc. Fast food is quick and easy to cook in large quantities, so it can be sold cheaply.

Fast food is sometimes called junk food. This makes it sound as if it fills you up without supplying any nutrients, which is not always true. Fast food is not bad for you unless you eat it very often and do not eat a variety of other food.

Nutritious take-aways

Some fast food is quite nutritious. Here are some examples.

Some fast foods and snacks contain a lot of fat and sugar. The red boxes show which you should not eat too often.

Chinese take-away food usually contains a lot of vegetables, and the fat content is low compared to other fast food.

A baked potato filled with coleslaw or grated cheese.

Fries are very fatty, although they also supply energy, protein and vitamin C.

Milkshakes contain a lot of sugar and fat, although they also contain some protein and calcium.

A hamburger made from lean meat in a wholemeal roll with salad.

A pizza with meat, vegetable and cheese on top.

A sausage roll is 36% fat.

Canteen fast food

Many school canteens serve fast food meals at lunchtime, though there is usually a salad choice. If you are going out for a hamburger and fries in the evening, have a salad at lunch so you do not eat too much fat.

So what is junk food?

Sweets, ice lollies, cheap cakes and biscuits, and sweet, fizzy drinks could be called junk food. Next time you buy a can of fizzy drink, look at the list of ingredients. Apart from sugar, it probably only contains flavourings and other additives. The sugar provides energy but nothing else, and it is bad for your teeth as you can see on the opposite page.

Food and your teeth

There is a close link between the amount of sweet food you eat and the number of fillings you need at the dentist. Here, you can find out how sugar causes tooth decay and what you can do to prevent it.

Sugar and tooth decay

Warmth + moisture + food = lots of bacteria

Bacteria can breed very fast inside your mouth. It is warm and moist and they feed on the tiny particles of food that remain in your mouth and coat your teeth. Sugar encourages the fastest bacterial growth.

Plaque building up around teeth.

As bacteria feed, they produce acid as a waste product. Your teeth become coated with a mess of sugar, breeding bacteria and acid. This is called plaque.

The acid in the plaque eats away at the enamel surface of your teeth.* When there is a hole in the enamel, the bacteria get inside. The hole gets larger and the tooth starts to decay.

You should go to the dentist at least twice a year.

When the decay hits a nerve, you get toothache. The dentist drills away the decayed part of the tooth and covers it with a filling.

Cleaning your teeth

Brushing your teeth removes bits of food from them which bacteria might feed on. It also gets rid of plaque but you need to brush for a good few minutes.

Change your toothbrush as soon as it starts to look worn.

Use a toothpaste that contains fluoride.*

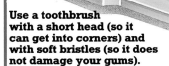

Use a toothbrush with a short head (so it can get into corners) and with soft bristles (so it does not damage your gums).

Cleaning your teeth after breakfast removes plaque that has built up overnight. Brushing last thing at night removes anything that might provide food for bacteria while you are asleep.

Avoiding tooth decay

Try not to eat too many sweets or sugary snacks between meals. Bacteria thrive best on sugar. Savoury foods are not bad for your teeth.

Sticky sweets such as toffees are very bad for your teeth. They stick to them and it is hard to remove all traces.

Have a drink of water after each meal to rinse your teeth and remove some of the food bacteria might feed on.

Did you know..?

★ In the UK, 80% of five year olds have some tooth decay.
★ Only one 12 year old in 200 has no fillings.
★ Dentists extract about four tonnes (four tons) of teeth from children each year.

* See page 10.

39

Food-related illnesses

Some people react badly to certain foods which are normally quite harmless. They are particularly sensitive to, or allergic to, substances in those foods. Other people, such as diabetics and coeliacs, do not have the usual ability to deal with certain food substances. These problems are described here. They can all be treated successfully.

Food allergies

1. Eggs.
2. Cows' milk.
3. Cheese.
4. Caffeine in coffee, coke etc.
5. Yeast extract.
6. Wine.
7. Bananas.
8. Oranges.
9. Certain food additives.

The substances to which people are most commonly allergic are found in the foods shown above.

Some people are born with food allergies but they may grow out of them as they get older.

Other people develop allergies during their lives, but these also might disappear later.

Allergy symptoms

Headache.

Skin rashes.

Runny nose.

Stomach pains, diarrhoea or constipation.

Feeling rotten.

People suffering from food allergies may get rashes, runny noses, stomach pains, diarrhoea, constipation, headaches, or just feel unwell. Symptoms appear up to several hours after eating the food. You may not realize they are due to an allergy as they are also symptoms of other mild illnesses.

Some hyperactive children* who are very restless, destructive and noisy have been diagnosed by doctors as being allergic to certain food additives.

Diagnosing food allergies

Restricted diet.

Different foods added one at a time . . .

. . . until a certain food produces an allergic reaction.

Diagnosing a food allergy must always be done under medical supervision, because it involves going on a strict diet. To start with, the diet only includes food to which people are very rarely allergic. Gradually, more foods are added to the diet one at a time to see when the allergy symptoms appear. The person then knows what foods cause his or her particular allergy and can avoid them.

40

*There is more about this on page 27.

What is diabetes?

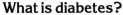

Glucose

PANCREAS

| Carbohydrates e.g. sugar are broken down into glucose. | Pancreas produces insulin which puts spare glucose into storage. | If there is little or no insulin, glucose has to be flushed out in urine. |

During digestion, carbohydrates are broken down into glucose.* The pancreas produces a substance called insulin which stores some of this glucose. People with diabetes (diabetics) produce little or no insulin. Excess glucose is got rid of in urine which requires a lot of water. Early symptoms of diabetes may be extreme thirst and a need to go to the toilet more than usual.

Developing diabetes

Some people are born with diabetes. Others may develop it as they grow older. It can also develop in people if they become very overweight. The pancreas gets worn out having to cope with a large carbohydrate intake.

Treatment of diabetes

Diabetes is usually treated with injections or tablets of insulin and a strict diet limiting sugar intake. Diabetes which appears in older people can sometimes be controlled by cutting down on sweet foods and controlling weight.

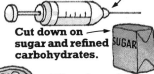
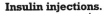

Insulin injections.

Cut down on sugar and refined carbohydrates.

SUGAR

Fibre slows down carbohydrate digestion.

BRAN

Less fat to limit risk of heart disease.

Eating fibre helps to control diabetes because fibre attaches itself to carbohydrates in your gut and slows down the rate at which they are absorbed. Diabetics should avoid too much fat and weight gain as they are more prone than others to heart disease.

Coeliac disease

Breakfast cereals made with wheat. Muesli containing oats.

Sausage and beefburgers to which breadcrumbs have been added.

Rye bread

Bread, cakes, pastries, biscuits and puddings made with wheat flour.

Canned soups containing wheat starch.

TOMATO SOUP

People with coeliac disease (coeliacs) are sensitive to a protein called gluten. It is found mainly in wheat, and in smaller amounts in rye, barley and oats. It damages the lining of a coeliac's small intestine, so food cannot be properly absorbed. The foods above contain gluten.

Treating coeliac disease

Many coeliacs grow out of the disease. If coeliacs stick to a diet that does not contain gluten, they can lead perfectly healthy lives. Some food companies make gluten-free bread, cakes and so on for coeliacs. People with undiagnosed coeliac disease are thin and prone to infection. They may go short of nutrients such as vitamins which they have been unable to absorb.

41

*There is more about digestion on pages 32-33.

Weight and weight control

People are all different shapes and sizes. If you look at pictures of models in magazines, though, or dummies in shop windows, they are always thin. There is a lot of pressure on people, especially girls and women, to be slim. Although to be overweight is not good for you, some crash diets are equally bad. People who try to stay below their natural weight are likely not to be as strong and fit as they could be.

Your body bank

Your body's fat stores are like money in the bank.

If you spend as much as you earn, there is none left to store in the bank.

If you earn more than you spend, you can save the rest in the bank.

When you spend more than you earn, you need to use up some of your savings.

Weight, fashion and your health

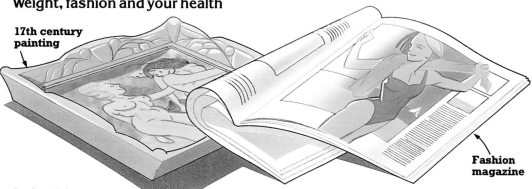

17th century painting

Fashion magazine

In the 17th century, it was fashionable for women to be curvy and fat. Nowadays, the fashion is to be very slim. Fashions have very little to do with what most people are like.

You need to be carrying quite a lot of extra fat around before it is bad for you. You do not need to be as skinny as models in fashion magazines.

My legs are killing me . . .

Being overweight puts a strain on some parts of your body. An overweight adult may suffer from pains in the back and joints, breathlessness and an overworked heart.

Being too thin can also be unhealthy. You may pick up infections more easily and feel weak and tired because you are not getting enough energy food. Dieting can become an obsession.

I haven't lost as much as last week . . .

If you are at all worried about whether you are too thin or too fat, go and see your doctor. The doctor may recommend a diet for you, or may reassure you that you are quite normal.

Using food energy

Some people eat a lot and never get fat. They use up food for energy more quickly than those who put on weight easily. The rate at which you convert food to energy is known as your metabolism.

Walking instead of catching the bus.

Dance or exercise classes.

Walking the dog.

Cycling to work or school.

Playing a sport.

Exercise can increase your metabolism. If you are trying to lose weight, get regular exercise and eat less fat and sugar. Doing any of the things in the picture regularly can increase your metabolism, use up calories* and keep you fit.

Using up extra calories

You may notice yourself feeling quite hot after a large meal.

You "burn off" some excess calories by producing body heat. This is called thermogenesis. Slim people probably burn off more calories in this way than people who tend to put on weight.

Without thermogenesis, you would get fatter and fatter if you regularly ate more calories than you needed for energy.

Although fat people appear to have more insulation on their bodies, they may feel the cold more than thin people. This is because thin people keep warmer through thermogenesis. It is like having your own mobile central heating system.

Losing weight

To lose weight, you need to cut down on foods which are high in calories but low in useful nutrients, such as fat** and sugar. You still need your daily requirement of protein, vitamins and minerals.

Cut down on . . .

1, Cakes   5, Pastries
2, Sweets   6, Chocolates
3, Biscuits   7, Sweet drinks
4, Puddings

Crash diets

A crash diet means dramatically reducing your calorie intake for a short time. You should not do it for more than a week without talking to your doctor about it. You may deprive yourself of vital minerals, proteins and vitamins.

— DIET SHEET —
Breakfast
Lunch
Supper

Crash diets are not as effective in the long run as slower ways of losing weight. You tend to put the weight back on as soon as you stop dieting. It is better to make changes in your eating habits which you can stick to for a longer period.

Fad diets

I never want to see another grape in my whole life.

Some diets tell you to eat only a limited range of food, such as tropical fruit or grapefruit. These only work as a way of reducing your calorie intake. No foods speed up the rate at which you use surplus body fat.

43

*Energy is measured in calories. See pages 6-7.
**See page 9.

Food charts

On the next few pages are some charts which show the nutritional value of different foods. On this page you can see what percentage of your daily needs are supplied by such things as a glass of milk or an egg. On the opposite page is a chart showing where most people get their nutrients.

Over the page there are charts showing which foods contain vitamins and minerals, and a reminder of what they do for you.

How much do these foods give you?

The figures in this chart show what percentage of your daily nutritional requirements are supplied by the foods in the left-hand column. The figures are based on the needs of boys and girls between the ages of 12 and 14. Boys usually grow more quickly than girls at this age, so they need more nutrients. The stars indicate that the food is a very important source of the nutrient.

The top figure is for a boy, the lower figure for a girl.	Energy	Protein	Vitamin B₁	Vitamin C	Calcium	Iron
Large glass of milk – one third of a litre (half a pint)	7%	14%	9%	12%	★49%	—
	9%	17%	11%	12%	★49%	—
Large slice of wholemeal bread	5%	8%	13%	—	2%	15%
	6%	10%	16%	—	2%	15%
113g (4oz) roast beef	10%	★32%	7%	—	—	17%
	12%	★39%	9%	—	—	17%
Medium-sized egg	3%	10%	4%	—	—	10%
	4%	13%	4%	—	—	10%
57g (2oz) hard cheese	9%	22%	2%	—	★66%	3%
	11%	27%	2%	—	★66%	3%
Medium-sized potato baked in jacket	4%	—	14%	★100%	—	13%
	5%	—	17%	★100%	—	13%
Orange	2%	—	11%	★225%	—	3%
	2%	—	13%	★225%	—	3%
85g (3oz) frozen peas	1%	6%	19%	★48%	—	8%
	2%	8%	23%	★48%	—	8%
Baked beans on one slice of toast	5%	13%	14%	16%	9%	21%
	6%	16%	17%	16%	9%	21%

Puzzle

From the chart above, you can see that if you ate all of these foods in one day you would have met all your protein needs, but not all your energy needs.

Using the information in this book, see if you can think of some other foods which would provide you with some extra energy. (Pages 6-7 might help you.)

Where do you get your nutrients?

The chart below shows which foods, on average, provide people with their nutrients. They show that a food rich in a certain nutrient may not be the main source, because it is not eaten very often.* The main supply of a nutrient may come from another food which is not so rich in it, but which is eaten in greater quantities.

The figures are averages derived from a National Food Survey carried out in the UK. If you are a vegetarian, for example, the figures will not apply to you.

"Cereal foods" in the charts include bread, flour, cakes, pastries, biscuits and breakfast cereals, plus other types of cereal food such as rice and pasta.

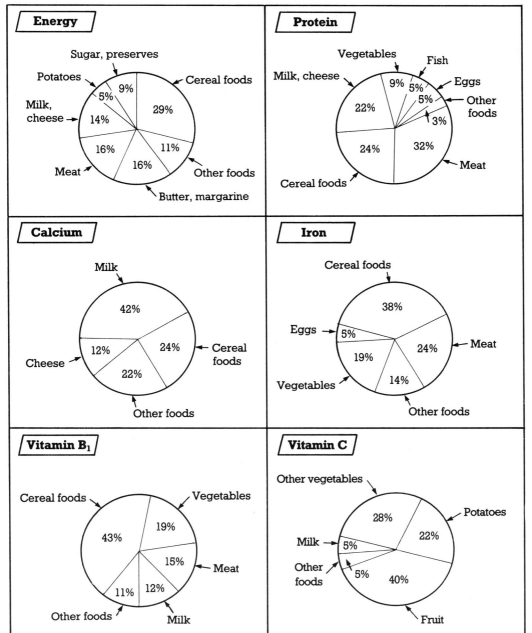

*You can find out which foods are richest in different nutrients over the page.

Vitamin chart

Here is a chart showing which foods are
richest in different vitamins, and what these
vitamins do for your body.

	Food sources	What vitamin does
Vitamin A (retinol)	Fish oils; liver; kidney; milk; butter; cheese; eggs; margarine; leafy green vegetables; yellow fruit e.g. apricots; carrots; tomatoes.	Maintains linings of tubes in body e.g. nose, gut. Keeps skin healthy – helps prevent spots. Helps you see in dim light. Essential for growth.
Vitamin B$_1$ (thiamin)	Pork; bacon; liver; kidney; wholegrain cereals; yeast; soya beans; fish; green vegetables e.g. peas; potatoes.	Helps body use carbohydrate (with B$_2$ and B$_3$). Tones muscles of digestive system. Helps digest protein. Keeps nerves healthy. Needed for growth.
Vitamin B$_2$ (riboflavin)	Milk; liver; yeast; wheatgerm; meat; soya beans; eggs; vegetables; nuts; dairy foods e.g. cheese.	Helps make digestive enzymes. Helps release energy from food. Essential for growth and general health. Keeps hair, skin, mouth and eyes healthy.
Vitamin B$_3$ (niacin)	Liver; lean meat; wholegrain cereals; vegetables e.g. green peppers, peas and potatoes; fish; poultry; yeast; peanuts; cheese; eggs.	Keeps skin and nervous system healthy. Helps digestion of carbohydrates and release of energy from food. Helps regulate cholesterol levels. Essential for growth.
Vitamin B$_5$ (pantothenic acid)	In most foods, especially: meat; cereal foods e.g. wholemeal bread and brown rice; vegetables; yeast; eggs; nuts.	Aids growth and body functions. Keeps skin, hair and other tissues healthy. Helps hair grow. Helps release energy from fat. Aids manufacture of nerve chemicals.
Vitamin B$_6$ (pyridoxine)	Meat; eggs; fish; cereals; green vegetables e.g. cabbage; yeast; wheatgerm and wholemeal products; milk.	Helps body use protein. Keeps skin, nerves and muscle healthy. Assists body functions. Makes hormones, enzymes and nerve chemicals.
Vitamin B$_{12}$ (cyanocobalamin)	Liver; meat; eggs; yeast extract; dairy foods; fish. (Absent in plant foods.)	Keeps nerves and skin healthy. Aids growth. Needed to make blood and new body cells. Helps body use protein.
Folic acid	Liver; offal meats; green vegetables; peas and beans; bread; bananas; wholegrain cereals; yeast.	Keeps blood healthy (works with vitamin B$_{12}$). Aids fertility. Essential for growth.
Biotin	Liver; kidney; egg yolk; oats; vegetables; nuts; wheatgerm.	Helps release energy from food.
Lecithin (choline and inositol)	Egg yolk; liver; kidney; wholegrain cereals; oats; peas and beans; nuts; wheatgerm.	General body maintenance. Helps liver function. Helps prevent build up of fats. A natural tranquillizer.
Vitamin C (ascorbic acid)	Citrus fruits e.g. oranges; green vegetables; tomatoes; potatoes; blackcurrants.	Keeps skin, blood vessels, gums, bones and teeth healthy. Helps heal wounds and bind cells. Helps resist infection. General body maintenance.
Vitamin D (calciferol)	Butter; margarine; eggs; fish liver oils; oily fish. Also produced by sunlight on skin.	Helps regulate absorption and distribution of calcium, so necessary for bones and teeth.
Vitamin E (tocopherol)	Seeds; leafy green vegetables; nuts; wholemeal bread; margarine; cereals; egg yolk; vegetable oil; wheatgerm.	Not fully understood, but you get anaemia if you are deficient. Protects body fats.
Vitamin K (phylioquinone)	Green vegetables; soya beans; liver; oils; cereals; fruit; nuts.	Helps clot blood.